Building Strong

Contents

Bridges carry people over water.
They carry trucks, cars, and trains.
Some bridges support buildings.
How do they hold
such heavy loads?

Stone Arch Bridge

Bridges with Arches

Look at this old bridge.
Arches have held it up for a
long, long time.
Shops line both sides
of the bridge.

**The Ponte Vecchio,
Florence, Italy**

3

**Sydney Harbor Bridge,
Sydney, Australia**

Look at this big bridge.
The arch is made of steel.
The road hangs on the steel arch.

This is the widest bridge in the world.
It has eight lanes for cars and trucks.
It also has two railroad tracks,
a bicycle path, and a walking path.

5

Suspension Bridges

Not all bridges are built with arches.
These bridges are held up by ropes.
They are suspension bridges.
A suspension bridge hangs
from ropes or cables.

**Bridge across
Rio Pastaza,
Ecuador**

Zanskar, India

6

Capilano Suspension Bridge,
Vancouver, B.C., Canada

This suspension bridge
is built with cables.
The cables are made of steel wires.
Wires are bundled and twisted together
to make strong cables.

**Brooklyn Bridge,
New York, NY**

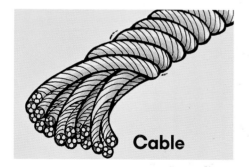

Cable

Bridges with Piers

Piers hold up this bridge.
The piers stand
on the bottom of the lake
like legs.

This is the longest bridge
in the world.
It is twenty-four miles
from end to end.

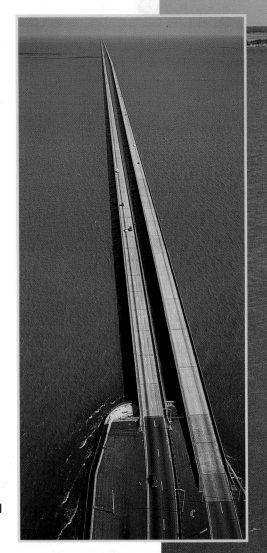

**Lake Pontchartrain
Causeway, Louisiana**

Build a Bridge

Let's build a bridge.

You'll need

- Heavy books (at least six)
- Manila tagboard
  (the kind file folders are
  made of)
- Scissors
- Ruler
- Toy car

Cut two tagboard strips.

Cut along the length of the tagboard.

Make a thin strip and a wide strip.

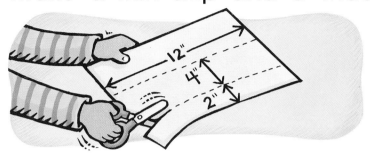

Stack the books in two equal piles.

Set them a few inches apart.

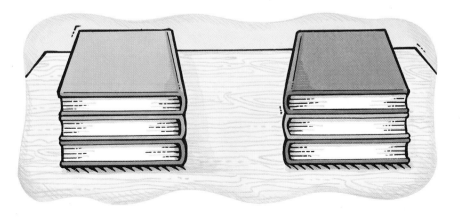

Lay the wide strip across the books.

It looks like a good bridge, doesn't it?

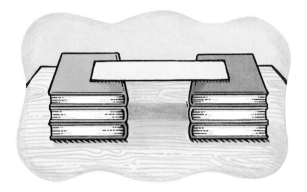

Now drive your car across it.

Uh oh! What happened?

Now make an arch.
Bend the thin strip of tagboard
between the piles of books.
Lay the wide strip across the top.

Drive your car over the bridge.
What did the arch do?

There are lots of ways to build bridges.
Why don't you try some more?